Komomo Confiserie

Volume 2

Story & Art by Maki Minami

MACARON

Komomo Confiserie

CONTENTS

I...I'M— I'M—!

I'M SORRY.

Komomo Confiserie

CHAPTER 6

• The Cover • ①

For this volume, I drew some macarons. The first macaron I ever ate was a pistachio one from the Sadaharu Aoki Patisserie. It was a delicious and moving experience for me. More recently, I really enjoyed the rose macarons from Pierre Hermé! I colored the cover to look like soft watercolor.

...SHE INVITED ME TO HER HOME.
OH, NATSU! MÉLI-MÉLO IS CLOSED WEDNESDAYS, RIGHT?
YOU WOULDN'T MIND IF I WENT TO RISE'S HOUSE AFTER SCHOOL ON THAT DAY, WOULD YOU?
RISE?
RISE... YOU MEAN THAT GIRL WHO WAS BULLYING YOU?
YES...
GO AND HAVE FUN.
TAKE THIS WITH YOU AS A GIFT.
WHAT IS IT?
SPOILED MEAT.
And tell her she can go to hell.
GRFF
WHY IS IT MOVING ?!
I'M JUST KIDDING.

I HOPE YOU GUYS BECOME GOOD FRIENDS.
FRIENDS.
YES.
I HOPE SO TOO.
WEDNESDAY, AFTER SCHOOL
WOW! WHAT A BEAUTIFUL OLD NEIGHBORHOOD!
UNLIKE YOUR DISTRICT, KOMOMO, THIS PLACE HAS HISTORY.
Well? Isn't it just the best?
TMP
TMP
AND OVER HERE IS–
WOW! WOULD YOU LOOK AT THAT, RISE?!
SHE'S NOT LISTENING TO ME!

• Greetings • (A)

Hello and nice to meet you! I'm Maki Minami, and this is volume 2 of *Komomo Confiserie.*

A lot of mangaka have turned to the digital medium for making their manga. Even though I use a computer for some things, I still draw on paper. But the screentones I use for the final stages of my drawings are not being produced as much, and there are fewer and fewer styles to choose from.

I guess there's nothing I can do about that...

WHITE DEER SWEET SHOP

A HORSE AND CARRIAGE!

OH, THERE ARE MANY OF THOSE AROUND HERE. THEY'RE USED FOR SIGHTSEEING.

My neighborhood is picture-perfect, right?

I LOVE HORSES.

WOULD IT BE ALL RIGHT IF I WERE TO RIDE YOUR HORSE, SIR?
HOLD IT!
TUG
FOR THE LOVE OF...! LISTEN WHEN PEOPLE ARE TALKING TO YOU!
WOW.
WHAT IS IT NOW?!
THIS IS THE FIRST TIME A GIRL HAS PULLED ME BY THE HAND AND WALKED WITH ME.
I RATHER LIKE IT!
WHITE DEER SWEET SHOP

THIS IS MY HOME.
SO NICE...
CASHIER
IT'S A TRADITIONAL SWEETS SHOP!
WELCOME HOME, MISTRESS RISE.
OH, DID YOU BRING A FRIEND?
THANK YOU FOR HAVING ME.
PLEASE, COME INSIDE. WE'LL BRING SOME TEA AND TASTY TREATS FOR YOU.

WOW.
THESE RAKUGAN ARE DELICIOUS.
MY FAMILY USED TO ORDER SWEETS LIKE THIS ALL THE TIME.
I SUPPOSE THEY CAME FROM YOUR FAMILY'S SHOP.
...
KLAK!!
LISTEN, KOMOMO-
MISTRESS RISE!
NEZU IS HERE!
NEZU ?!

IS HE A FRIEND OF YOURS?
N-NO, NOT THAT.
BLUSH
TEE HEE. NOT QUITE.
HE'S A COLLEGE STUDENT WHO COMES EVERY WEDNESDAY.
MISTRESS RISE ADMIRES HIM GREATLY.
SHIBA!!
OH.
GLINT
GLINT
HELLO, RISE.
SO RISE AND THIS BOY...
HMPH.

SO YOU CAME AGAIN, DARING TO SHOW YOUR TAWDRY FACE TO ME?
I ADMIRE YOUR COURAGE.
?!!
I'M SORRY, BUT THE SWEETS HERE ARE JUST TOO DELICIOUS.
BLUSH
BESIDES, I LIKE SEEING YOUR PRETTY FACE.
I CAN'T HELP BUT KEEP COMING BACK.
HMPH!!
SATISFIED? IF YOU'VE BOUGHT WHAT YOU WANTED, JUST LEAVE!
OKAY. I'LL COME AGAIN.
HMPH!
RISE...
WHITE DEER SWEET SHOP
DON'T YOU THINK HE MIGHT NOT LIKE YOU VERY MUCH IF YOU ACT THAT WAY...
...RISE?
I KNOW THAT!

YOU CAN RELATE, RIGHT? YOU'VE BEEN IN LOVE BEFORE, HAVEN'T YOU?
I'VE ALWAYS BEEN TOLD THERE'S NO REASON FOR ME TO FALL IN LOVE.
BUT THE MORE I LIKE SOMEONE, THE MORE NERVOUS I GET. I SAY THINGS I DON'T MEAN!
MY FUTURE HUSBAND WAS DECIDED FOR ME WHEN I WAS VERY YOUNG.
I'VE NEVER SEEN HIM, AND I DON'T EVEN KNOW HIS NAME.

I DON'T KNOW MUCH ABOUT LOVE.
BUT IF THERE'S ANYTHING I CAN DO TO HELP, JUST LET ME KNOW.
I WANT TO...
...BE YOUR FRIEND, RISE.
...!

I...
I'm...
...
ACK!
DON'T BE AN IDIOT!
?!!
YOU'VE LOST YOUR SOCIAL STANDING, REMEMBER?
YOU'VE LOST EVERYTHING.
THAT MEANS YOUR ARRANGED MARRIAGE IS OVER WITH TOO!
SO...

...YOU CAN LOVE WHOMEVER YOU WANT TO NOW.
WHOMEVER I WANT...
OH...
I CAN LOVE FREELY.

I'LL SUPPORT YOU IN YOUR PURSUIT OF LOVE! THAT WAY I CAN LEARN ABOUT IT TOO!
KLASP
IS THERE ANYTHING I CAN DO?
N-NEXT WEDNESDAY...
...IS NEZU'S BIRTHDAY.
I WANT TO GET HIM SOMETHING NICE, BUT...
...WHAT SHOULD I GET?
SOMETHING NICE...

I HAVE JUST THE THING!
IE MELI-MELO
CONFISERIE
méli-mélo
Traiteur
Epicerie
Specialites
WELL, WELL. IF IT ISN'T HER HIGHNESS.
YOU'RE THE QUEEN BEE WHO STARTED TORMENTING KOMOMO-SAMA ON THE VERY FIRST DAY OF SCHOOL.
WHAT BRINGS SUCH ROYALTY TO MY HUMBLE SHOP?
Your Majesty!
BECAUSE I HAVE NOTHING TO SELL YOU.
I WON'T LET YOU BULLY MY FRIEND!
OH, I'M JUST JOKING AROUND.
I... I'M SORRY...
NATSU!

YOU'RE HERE TO ORDER A BIRTHDAY CAKE?

SHE NEEDS A CAKE THAT WILL MAKE HER LOVE COME TRUE.

IF NEZU EATS ONE OF NATSU'S CAKES...

...HE'S SURE TO UNDERSTAND HOW YOU FEEL ABOUT HIM.

...

IS IT REALLY?

CONFISERIE MEL

SO, YOU'RE GIVING HER LOVE ADVICE, KOMOMO-SAMA?

THAT'S CORRECT, NATSU. GIVING LOVE ADVICE IS FUN.

GARBAGE BAG

SAY, NATSU.

I'M THINKING I'D LIKE TO FALL IN LOVE TOO!
I WANT TO FIND A GOOD MAN.
HMM.
OKAY. HOW ABOUT ME?

BECAUSE YOU BITE MY EARS!
OH.

NO...!
NEVER!!

THAT'S TOO BAD.
NATSU!
HE'S TEASING ME AGAIN!!
SUDDENLY IT'S WEDNESDAY.
HERE'S THE PLAN, RISE.
UNTIL I ARRIVE WITH THE CAKE...
...BE SURE TO STALL NEZU FOR AS LONG AS YOU CAN IN THE SHOP.
R-RIGHT.
THANK YOU. I'LL DO MY BEST!

THANK YOU.
THE CREATION IS AN ISPAHAN...
...A MACARON CAKE SHAPED LIKE A HEART AND SPRINKLED WITH ROSE PETALS.
meli-melo
I WILL RUN...
...FOR MY FRIEND WHO IS IN LOVE.
HOW STRANGE. EVEN THOUGH I'M RUNNING SO FAR, I'M NOT TIRED.
I WONDER WHY THAT IS.

BUT WHEN I ARRIVED AT THE SHOP...

...I FOUND RISE DEPRESSED AND SLUMPED OVER ON THE FLOOR.

APPARENTLY HE'S ALREADY ON HIS WAY BACK TO THE STATION.

IT'S OVER...

I'LL DO MY BEST.
DIDN'T YOU MEAN IT WHEN YOU SAID...
...YOU'D DO YOUR BEST?
IS LOVE SOMETHING...
...YOU CAN GIVE UP ON SO EASILY?
...
NO, IT'S NOT...
IN THAT CASE...

DON'T GIVE UP!
Méli-Mélo
I'LL GO FETCH HIM FROM THE STATION.
JUST GET READY AND WAIT HERE UNTIL I GET BACK.

HUH...?
YOU THERE!
LEND ME YOUR STEED!

Méli-Mélo
BIENVENUE
WHAT...
...AM I DOING?
IN THE END...
MRMR
MRMR
CHATTER

...I SAFELY CAUGHT NEZU.
SNORT

I WAS SCOLDED BY THE CARRIAGE DRIVER A SHORT WHILE LATER.

I can't believe I let you take my horse! How could you do that to me? Are you a general? Who are you?

AND AS FOR RISE...

IT ALL WORKED OUT...

SHE WAS ABLE TO GIVE THE CAKE TO NEZU.
LISTEN, NATSU.
NEZU SAID SINCE NEXT WEDNESDAY IS A HOLIDAY...
...HE'S GOING TO TAKE RISE TO THE MOVIES TO THANK HER FOR THE CAKE.
BUT RISE IS STILL A LITTLE NERVOUS ABOUT GOING ON HER OWN...
...SO I'LL BE GOING AS WELL.
GO ENJOY YOURSELF, BUT DON'T BECOME A THIRD WHEEL.
YOU DON'T HAVE TO WORRY.
HUH. WELL, GOOD JOB.
★TODAY'S SWEET★
SAKURA MOCHI, COURTESY OF RISE
WHY IS THAT?
HEH HEH HEH. BECAUSE...

NEZU IS BRINGING ALONG ONE OF HIS MALE FRIENDS TOO.

NOW THEN...

IT'LL BE WHAT IS CALLED A "DOUBLE DATE."

I'M SO EXCITED!

HA HA HA...

YEAH. I'M EXCITED ABOUT IT TOO...

SHATTER

I WONDER HOW IT WILL GO.

CHAPTER 7

② • Drama CD •

A drama CD of chapters 1–4 has been made!
I even got to go to the studio for the post-recording session. All the voice actors had the characters down pat, which made me super happy. But I felt a little bad about how difficult the pronunciation of some of the pastries are. Still, I loved that they asked me, "Is his name 'Natsu' because it sounds like 'nuts'?" They hit the nail on the head! It was a really fun session!!

OH... THIS IS MY CELL PHONE!
I PUT MY NUMBER IN THE ADDRESS BOOK.
IF ANYTHING HAPPENS ON YOUR DOUBLE DATE TOMORROW, GIVE ME A CALL.
WHAT WOULD HAPPEN?
...
LOOK, KOMOMO-SAMA...
...THERE ARE SOME GUYS WHO ARE UP TO NO GOOD.
THERE ARE BAD PEOPLE IN THE WORLD.
YES...
UNBELIEVABLE.
IT'S A GOOD THING WE AGREED TO MEET UP AN HOUR BEFORE OUR DATES ARRIVE.

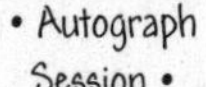

• Autograph Session • (B)

On December 1, 2013, I held an autograph session in the Marui Annex in Shinjuku!! The huge turnout made me so happy! Thank you to everyone who came! And meeting people who had been to past autograph sessions of mine was amazing! I would ask this question...

...only to be told...

I wish I knew how to give witty comebacks.

Oh, never mind.

SO THIS IS WHAT PEOPLE WEAR ON DATES.
PHOO
I CAN'T BELIEVE IT.
SUCH A HASSLE.
SIGH
BUT IT'S A LITTLE TIGHT AROUND THE CHEST.
YEAH, YEAH, YOU'RE WELL-ENDOWED!
I knew you'd say that.
THIS IS KOMOMO NINOMIYA. SHE'S A FORMER RICH GIRL WHO IS COMPLETELY IGNORANT OF THE WAYS OF THE WORLD.
And this part is awfully short.
I WAS SURPRISED TO LEARN THIS WILL BE HER FIRST DATE EVER.
EVEN THOUGH I WAS MEAN TO HER IN THE PAST, SHE'S COME THROUGH FOR ME TWICE ALREADY.
I HOPE EVERYTHING WORKS OUT BETWEEN YOU AND NEZU TODAY...
...RISE!

I WISH I COULD JUST SMILE AND AGREE.

IF I TRY HARD AND THINGS GO WELL WITH NEZU TODAY...

...I WANT TO SMILE AT HER AND SAY THANK YOU.

OOOOH!

NICE GOING, NEZU! THEY'RE BOTH WICKED CUTE!

SO WHICH ONE IS MY DATE?

KNOCK IT OFF, TAISHI. YOU'RE SCARING THEM.
RISE IS THE ONE I ASKED OUT ON A DATE.
RIGHT?
I-I DON'T REALLY CARE WHICH ONE OF YOU IT IS!
HMPH!
WHY DID I SAY THAT?!
OKAY. BUT I'D LIKE TO BE WITH YOU, RISE.
NEZU IS ALWAYS LIKE THIS.
EVEN WHEN I SHOUT AT HIM, HE ALWAYS SMILES AND IS STILL KIND TO ME.

THAT'S HOW I FELL FOR HIM.
THIS...
...IS A MOVIE THEATRE!
CINEMA NUEVE
Bain-marie
fouet
assiette creuse
NOW ON
I'VE NEVER BEEN TO ONE BEFORE!
Huh?
THIS IS YOUR FIRST TIME, KOMOMO-CHAN?
Ah?
YES, IT IS.
HM?
BECAUSE WE HAD A THEATRE IN OUR HOUSE.
SHOCK
HM?
SNIFF
Popcorn
Butter
Caramel
Honey
Strawberry
S ¥450
M ¥550
L ¥600
I SMELL CARAMEL POPCORN!

OUR PÂTISSIER WOULD MAKE IT FOR US WHEN WE WOULD WATCH A MOVIE!

UH...

DO YOU COME FROM A RICH FAMILY OR SOMETHING, KOMOMO?

OH, THAT'S ALL IN THE PAST.

NOW I SPEND EACH DAY WORKING FOR SWEETS AND ¥500.

LOOK!!

BUT NATSU GAVE ME A SPECIAL BONUS TODAY. ¥3,000!

Y-YEAH, THAT'S GREAT...

Heh heh. Pretty impressive, isn't it?

*ABOUT $30

HOW ABOUT I BUY YOU SOME POPCORN?

AH!

I'LL BUY IT!

I'VE GOT TO SHOW THAT I HAVE A GOOD SIDE TOO.

Ah, Rise?

...

BUT STILL...

SHE WORKS ALL DAY FOR SWEETS AND A MEASLY ¥500?
I WONDER IF AZUMI IS TAKING ADVANTAGE OF HER.
Welcome.
BECAUSE I HAVE NOTHING TO SELL YOU.
HEH HEH HEH
HE SEEMS THE TYPE!
TNK

HERE'S MY SHARE. I HOPE IT'S ENOUGH.
WAIT...!
IT'S ON ME, SO I DON'T NEED THAT.
Please come again!
HUH? BUT–
Besides, it's not enough!

THANK YOU, RISE!

YES.

I WANT TO...

...SHOW HIM MORE AND MORE...

...OF MY GOOD SIDE.

I THINK I COULD REALLY USE THIS.
HEY, THIS IS NICE!
WINNIR ROAD
LAPAZ BLUE
OH, THEIR LATEST ALBUM IS OUT.
New
LAPAZ BLUE
HUH? FOR ME? THANKS!
BUT I DON'T HAVE ENOUGH MONEY FOR IT THIS MONTH.
New Release
GUESS I'LL JUST HAVE TO WAIT...
New Release
Cashier
YOU GOT IT FOR ME? THANKS!!
Huh?
Hey, Komomo! You listening to me?
...
Food Chain

HEY, RISE.

IS TODAY NEZU'S BIRTHDAY?

NO. DON'T YOU REMEMBER THAT I GAVE HIM THE CAKE LAST WEEK?

THEN WHY ARE YOU BUYING HIM SO MANY PRESENTS?

IF YOU GIVE TOO MANY PRESENTS, THEY WON'T SEEM SPECIAL.

I DON'T THINK IT'S A GOOD THING.

AND THE WAY NEZU JUST ACCEPTS THEM OR EVEN ASKS YOU OUTRIGHT FOR THEM...

WHAT HAS HE GIVEN YOU IN RETURN?

HIS...
HIS SMILE.
YOU DON'T KNOW ANYTHING.
GRIP
SO STAY OUT OF IT.
I WONDER IF I SAID SOMETHING WRONG.
BUT IF SHE KEEPS DOING THIS...
KOMOMO?
OH YEAH, YOU'RE THE IDIOT WHOSE FAMILY LOST IT ALL.

SHE'LL END UP LIKE ME.
DO YOU THINK KOMOMO-CHAN WILL BE ALL RIGHT?
YOU HAVE TODAY OFF TOO. YOU SHOULD'VE GONE WITH HER.
NO WAY.
BUT YOU'VE BEEN RESTLESS ALL DAY, AND YOU KEEP CHECKING YOUR PHONE.
EITHER WAY, I CAN'T LEAVE.
And even if I could, I wouldn't.
...YEAH, I GUESS YOU'RE RIGHT.
WE GOT A BIG ORDER IN YESTERDAY FROM THE "PRINCESS" OF FRANCE.
AT LEAST KOMOMO-CHAN CAN BE WITH HER FRIENDS.
SHE SHOULD BE FINE.

WHY DID SHE SAY THAT?
KOMOMO DOESN'T KNOW WHAT SHE'S TALKING ABOUT.
SALE
SALE
I'VE GIVEN NEZU A LOT OF PRESENTS, BUT...
BUT...
...I'VE BEEN SO TERRIBLE TO HIM THAT I MUST DO THIS.
WOW, NEZU.
RISE SURE IS CRAZY ABOUT YOU.
YEAH, I GUESS.
SHE USED TO PLAY HARD-TO-GET, BUT NOW SHE'S JUST TOO EASY.
EASY...?
UH-OH.

HEY. YOU'RE BACK, RISE.

That was fast.

DOES HE ACTUALLY THINK I'M EASY?

SAY, RISE.

WANT TO GO TO KARAOKE AFTER THIS?

I CAN'T BELIEVE IT.

S-SURE.

NEZU...

I DON'T THINK...
...IT'S A GOOD THING.
IT CAN'T BE...
Sundays & Mondays ☆ Double Service
Get a Discount with Ocean Points!
Discount! 10% Off Your Karaoke Experience!
KARAOKE
OOH! SHISHIGU
THEY WOULDN'T...

THEY WOULD.
SINCE YOU OVERHEARD US EARLIER, WE'VE HAD TO ACCELERATE OUR SCHEDULE.
NEZU COMPLETELY FOOLED ME.
NOW THAT WE HAVE YOU HERE...
...WE'RE GOING TO TAKE SOME EMBARRASSING PHOTOS OF YOU.
UM...
NEZU, DO YOU MEAN...
...THAT YOU ONLY GOT CLOSE TO RISE...
...SO THAT YOU COULD ASK HER ON A DATE, INVITE HER TO KARAOKE...
...AND TAKE SCANDALOUS PHOTOGRAPHS TO BLACKMAIL HER FOR MONEY?
NEZU...
IS THAT RIGHT?
EXACTLY.
...WAS ONLY AFTER MY MONEY.
THIS KARAOKE PLACE IS UNDER THE PATRONAGE OF OUR CIRCLE.
So there's no use screaming for help.
YOUR CIRCLE?

WE'RE CALLED THE "SCORE US AN ATM GIRL" OR "OUR ATM" FOR SHORT.

We're the two only people in it. ☆

SHLLP

THIS IS REALLY BAD.

THAT'S A CRIME!

AND YOU'RE OUR FIRST TARGET. THIS IS SOMETHING TO COMMEMORATE.

Are you listening, Komomo?

SHLLP

This drink doesn't taste very good.

HEY.

BIP

BIP

WHAT ARE YOU DOING?

NATSU TOLD ME TO CALL HIM IF ANYTHING HAPPENED.

SNATCH

WHO DO YOU THINK YOU ARE? CALLING FOR HELP RIGHT IN FRONT OF US?!

OH

WHO DO I THINK I AM?

WHO DO YOU THINK YOU ARE?

YOU DARE TRY TO BLACKMAIL ME AND MY FRIEND?

JOLT

IF YOU THINK I'M GOING TO LET YOU...

...TRICK MY FRIEND AND GET AWAY WITH IT–

I FEEL INTIMIDATED...

REEL

FLOP
KOMOMO ?!
I GUESS IT WORKED.
WE PUT SLEEPING PILLS IN YOUR DRINKS.
TOO BAD FOR YOU.
AN ILL-NATURED GIRL LIKE YOU ACTUALLY MADE A FRIEND...
HE'S RIGHT.
I'M ILL-NATURED AND TWISTED.
...BUT NOW YOU'LL HAVE TO WATCH HER SUFFER.

SUFFER?
BUT...
...I DECIDED TO CHANGE.
I WANT TO...
...BE YOUR FRIEND, RISE.
SHE'LL SUFFER...
CHILLS
...BECAUSE OF ME?

I'LL NEVER...

...LET THAT HAPPEN.

HEH.

...MAKE ME LAUGH.

THE MOMENT I TOOK OUT MY PURSE, YOU FOLLOWED ME LIKE LITTLE PUPPIES.
THAT'S RIGHT.
I SUSPECTED THAT YOU MIGHT BE DUMB...
...AND YOU DID EXACTLY AS I THOUGHT YOU WOULD.
I CAN BE VERY WICKED.

YOU'RE SO PREDICTABLE. IT MAKES ME LAUGH.
WHAT DID YOU SAY?!
DID I UPSET YOU?
HEH HEH. NOW THEN...
OH.
YOU THERE.
THAT'S HOW I KNOW...
YOU'LL ONLY EVER GET NEZU'S LEFTOVERS.
YOU CAN'T DO ANYTHING ON YOUR OWN.
HEH HEH
YOU'RE LOWER THAN A HYENA.
...I CAN STIR THEM UP.
HEE
BLUSH

DASH
I KNOW WHAT TO SAY TO DRIVE THEM OVER THE EDGE.
YOU–!
I NEED TO BUY TIME...
...SO I CAN SUMMON HELP.
BUT I'M NOT FINDING AN OPENING.
BONK
FLING
NOW I'M REALLY MAD!
I'M GOING TO BEAT THE CRAP OUT OF YOU!
I DON'T CARE.

I DON'T CARE.
BAM!!
I'VE BEEN HORRIBLE TO ALL SORTS OF PEOPLE IN MY LIFE.

THAT'S WHY...

HUFF

HUFF

HUFF
HUFF

YOU BASTARDS...
SHOCK
WHAT DID YOU DO TO HER?
I DON'T CARE WHAT HAPPENS TO ME.

CHAPTER 8
NATSU...
...CAME TO THE RESCUE OF KOMOMO AND HER FRIEND.
WELL?

ARE YOU THE ONES...
...WHO DID THIS TO KOMOMO-SAMA?
WHO IS THIS GUY?
I'm scared.
NATSU!
KOMOMO IS ONLY ASLEEP. SHE'S FINE.
JUST GET HER OUT OF HERE!
HUH?
I'LL TAKE CARE OF THE REST.
...
③
Hmm, what should I do?
Maybe I won't do anything...
#1

SHK
PLIP
SHK
PLIP
SHK
YOU'RE TREMBLING.
I KNOW SELF-DEFENSE. I'LL BE FINE!
HUH.
HEY, NATSU!
HUFF
HUFF
HUFF
HUFF
DID YOU FIND KOMOMO?
WHEEZE
YURI.
TAKE KOMOMO-SAMA AND THIS GIRL SOMEWHERE SAFE.
AH, RIGHT.
Okay.
HOLD IT! WHAT DO YOU GUYS THINK YOU'RE DOING?!
You band of chefs!
GLARE
HAH?!
JOLT
I'LL TAKE CARE OF THESE GUYS ON MY OWN.
SILENCE
NOW THEN.

THP
I'LL MAKE YOU REGRET...
...EVER COMING NEAR KOMOMO-SAMA!
YOU TOOK COMPROMISING PHOTOS OF THEM AND THREATENED TO MAKE THEM PUBLIC IF THEY EVER TRIED ANY-THING LIKE THIS AGAIN?
SO.
YEP.

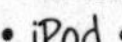

I've been lending my friend Mno-chan my old iPod for a long time. One day it stopped working, so she ran to her older brother for help.

Mno's brother is good with electronics and fixed it. Then he took a look at what's on it and said...

IT'S SO NOISY...
I HOPE RISE IS OKAY.
NEZU IS A CRUEL PERSON.
EVEN THOUGH RISE LIKED HIM...
AH...
I WASN'T ABLE TO HELP RISE IN HER PURSUIT OF LOVE AFTER ALL.
OH.

KOMOMO, YOU'RE AWAKE.

B-BMP

JOLT

?!

N-NATSU?! AND YURI? RISE TOO!

HUH? WHERE AM I...?

W...

WHAT?

GLOW
I'M JUST GLAD.

HUG
...
NATSU?
...
KOMOMO.
OH
RISE! YOU'RE ALL RIGHT!
I'M SO SORRY, KOMOMO!
RISE?
IT'S ALL MY FAULT YOU WERE PUT IN DANGER.

IT'S NOT YOUR FAULT, RISE-SAN.
IF ANYONE SHOULD BE APOLOGIZING, IT'S ME.
I'M SORRY I COULDN'T HELP YOU FIND LOVE.
S...
SILLY!
THAT DOESN'T MATTER. HE WAS A TERRIBLE GUY TO HAVE A CRUSH ON. LOVE IS CRUEL...

I...
I...
BLUSH
I...!
I'M MUCH HAPPIER KNOWING WE'VE BECOME FRIENDS, KOMOMO!
I HAVE A SONG TO SING YOU AS A PRESENT!
HUH?
UM.
A song?
FRIENDS.
AAH
K- KOMOMO?

"Lacrimosa dies illa, qua resurget ex favilla"
Y-YOU REALLY ARE SINGING!
You're good too...
MRMR
WHEN SHE TOLD ME SHE WAS HAPPY TO BE MY FRIEND...
カメラ
MRMR
MRMR
...IT MADE ME HAPPY TOO.
"judicandus homo reus:"
"Huic ergo parce Deus. Pie Jesu Domine,"
What's going on?
What is this song?
Opera?
"Dona eis requiem. Amen."
I WANT TO SHARE THIS FEELING WITH RISE.

THE END.
WHERE DID THAT COME FROM?!
KLAP
BOW
I WANTED TO SING A REQUIEM TO YOU...
...FOR BEING MY FRIEND.
ARE YOU TRYING TO PUT MY SOUL TO REST?!
A REQUIEM IS ALSO SUNG TO BRING RELIEF.
I HOPE HEARING IT REFRESHES YOUR HEART.
LOVE WILL NO LONGER BE CRUEL.
BECAUSE...
...NEXT TIME YOU'LL FIND SOMEONE GREAT TO LOVE.

NEXT TIME...
...YOU'LL FIND SOMEONE GREAT TO LOVE.
SEE YOU LATER.
THANKS FOR WALKING RISE HOME.
I'LL WALK KOMOMO BACK.

I'M SURE I WILL.
THIS GUY...
...IS OLDER THAN NATSU AZUMI, BUT HE STILL WORKS UNDER HIM?
He takes orders from him.
THAT WAS IMPRESSIVE.
4-chome Miko ~ Miko Honm
1-chome Mikamo
WHAT WAS?
THE WAY YOU PROTECTED KOMOMO UNTIL NATSU SHOWED UP.
TMP
THANKS.

PAT
BUT DON'T BE TOO RECKLESS WITH YOUR SAFETY.
...I WON'T.
...
NATSU... ARE YOU ANGRY?

...
DO YOU REMEMBER THE WARNING I GAVE YOU, KOMOMO-SAMA?
HUH?
...
THERE ARE SOME GUYS WHO ARE UP TO NO GOOD.
YOU WERE RIGHT ABOUT THAT.
Wow! Those two really were up to no good!
I'M SURE YOU GET IT NOW.
SO BE MORE CAREFUL IN THE FUTURE.
GLARE
JOLT
I WILL...
NATSU...
THANK YOU...
...FOR COMING TO RESCUE US.

IF YOU EVER NEED RESCUING AGAIN...
...I'LL COME WHENEVER YOU NEED ME.
BECAUSE...
...I DON'T WANT ANYONE ELSE TORMENTING MY KOMOMO-SAMA.

OH, AND ALSO...
...SINCE YOUR FIRST DATE WAS A DISASTER...
...HOW ABOUT DOING IT OVER?
WITH YOU?
YOU DON'T WANT TO BECAUSE I BITE YOUR EAR, RIGHT?
THEN LET'S GO ON A DATE.
A-AS LONG AS YOU DON'T BITE, I'M OKAY WITH IT.
GOOD.

IT'S ALREADY NIGHTTIME.

SO WE CAN'T DO THE FULL DAY COURSE.

IF IT EVEN COULD BE CALLED A DATE...

BUT WE CAN ENJOY A TASTY DINNER AND DESSERT—JUST THE TWO OF US.

MY FIRST DOUBLE DATE...

...WAS NEW AND DIFFERENT IN MANY WAYS.

IT WASN'T WHAT I THOUGHT A DATE SHOULD BE LIKE.

THE DATES I'VE READ ABOUT IN NOVELS...

...ARE EXCITING AND MAKE YOUR HEART RACE.

ATO, HAM, AND
EESE QUICHE
450
HAMBURGER WITH
CHEESH TOMATO
NEXT UP IS DESSERT.
THERE'S A SHOP I'VE BEEN MEANING TO CHECK OUT, SO LET'S STOP IN ON OUR WAY.
OKAY!

Chateaubriant
Chateaubriant
YES...
IT'S JUST AS FUN AS I IMAGINED IT WOULD BE.
IT'S BEAUTIFUL.

YOU CAN SEE THE ENTIRE CITY FROM UP HERE.
THAT'S WHY...
...I STARTED THINKING ABOUT IT.
TRY THIS ÉCLAIR.
IT'S PARTICULARLY GOOD WITH THIS BACKDROP.
MNCH MNCH
THIS IS DELICIOUS.
AND THIS VIEW MAKES IT ALL THE MORE SO.
I THINK SO TOO.

I KNEW IT. THE SWEETS YOU MAKE ARE THE BEST OF ALL, NATSU.
WELL, THANKS.
I'M GLAD TO HEAR THAT.
...
I...

SAY, NATSU.
I THINK WHEN IT COMES TO DATING, IT'S BETTER TO MAKE IT FUN. DON'T YOU THINK?
YEAH, I AGREE.
I...
I'M HAVING A LOT OF FUN ON THIS DATE WITH YOU.
YOU CAN LOVE WHOMEVER YOU WANT TO NOW.
I'VE
ECIDED.

OKAY. HOW ABOUT ME?
I...
...WANT TO FALL IN LOVE.
WHAT IS ONE SUPPOSED TO DO ON A DATE AFTER EATING?
IF I REMEMBER CORRECTLY...
...THE NOVELS I'VE READ ALWAYS MENTION...
SKOOK
THAT'S WHY...
NATSU.

MWAAH
THAT'S WHY...
KLUP

MOOOOOSH
WHAT ARE YOU DOING?
MMMPH!

WHAT ELSE?
Ouch!
I'M TRYING TO KISS YOU.

I'VE DECIDED.
...
WHY?

BECAUSE I'VE MADE UP MY MIND.
ABOUT WHAT?

LOOK, NATSU...

...I WANT TO FALL IN LOVE WITH YOU.
IF I'M GOING TO LOVE ANYONE, I WANT IT TO BE HIM.

CHAPTER 9

"Komomo Confiserie"
Stage Data Corner!!
Most of the backgrounds I use are made using a 3-D modeler. With this, I can draw a setting from any angle I want! It's really handy!
ly assistant
ou-san made this
or me! Besides the
hop, there's the
itchen, back patio,
nd the second floor
f Méli-Mélo. It's so
un to spin the 3-D
odel around and
round!
Méli-Mélo as seen from above.
Méli-Mélo
BIENVENUE
Second floor of Méli-Mélo. Komomo typically eats her treats here with Natsu.

BACK WHEN I WAS LIVING IN THAT HOUSE, I WAS ALWAYS TOLD THAT THERE WAS NO NEED FOR ME TO FIND LOVE.
I THOUGHT LOVE WAS SOMETHING THAT ONLY EXISTED IN FAIRY TALES.
BUT NOW I'M FREE...
4
I can't think of anything to talk about that will fit this 1/4 panel space!
Yeah!
#2

...I WANT TO FALL IN LOVE.
NATSU...
...I WANT TO FALL IN LOVE WITH YOU.
IF I'M GOING TO LOVE ANYONE...
...
SMILE
OKAY, SURE.
...I WANT IT TO BE HIM.

LET'S FALL IN LOVE.
I'M ABSOLUTELY SURE...
...THAT LOVE IS THE DRAMATIC, ROMANTIC AND WONDERFUL THING YOU SEE IN NOVELS AND MOVIES.
AND NOW AT LAST...
...I WILL EXPERIENCE IT FOR MYSELF!
CONFISERIE
meli-melo
Traiteur
Epicerie
Specialites
UM...

WE STARTED GOING OUT LAST NIGHT.
O-OKAY.
I'LL KILL YOU IF YOU TRY TO MAKE A PASS AT HER.
AND WITH THAT, PLEASE SUPPORT US.
THAT WAS GLORIOUS, NATSU!
WHEN YOU SAID, "I'LL KILL YOU IF YOU TRY TO MAKE A PASS AT HER," IT FELT LIKE SOMETHING FROM A MOVIE!
I KNOW, RIGHT?
NOW THEN, KOMOMO-SAMA. IT'S NEARLY TIME TO OPEN, SO PLEASE PREPARE THE SHOP FOR YOUR LOVER'S SAKE.
OH, I WILL!

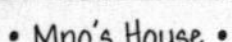

Ⓓ

My friend Mno-chan is the type who brings out the sun. When we travel together, chances are we'll have nice weather. This is the story of when we went on a bus tour to Lake Mashu in Hokkaido.

It was raining cats and dogs.

The tour guide said...

Rain is good for Lake Mashu.

And it's especially good for the single ladies out there.

If the sun comes out on Lake Mashu, they say you'll marry late in life.

So aren't we lucky it's raining?

But the moment we arrived... No joke, the sun came out.

SWISH

I'll be right back, darling.

KOMOMO-SAMA SUDDENLY TOLD ME SHE WANTED TO FALL IN LOVE WITH ME, SO...

UH... WAS ALL THAT TRUE?

YES. ISN'T IT AMUSING?

I'VE DECIDED TO USE MY BODY TO TEACH HER WHAT LOVE IS ABOUT.
S-SOME-THING...
...ABOUT THE WAY YOU SAY THAT IS A LITTLE SCARY.
AND NOW...
CONFISERIE MÉLI-MÉLO
Confiserie
Traiteur
...FOR MY LOVE WITH NATSU...
KOMOMO-SAMA.
IT'S A LITTLE MESSY OUT THERE. WOULD YOU CLEAN IT UP FOR YOUR DARLING?
WOULD YOU TAKE OUT THE TRASH FOR YOUR LOVE?

THE WORKDAY IS OVER, BUT I'VE GOT TO FIGURE OUT THIS SUMMER'S RECIPES.

SO WOULD YOU POUR ME A CUP OF TEA?

FOR YOUR DARLING?

D...

DARLING, MY FOOT!

THWAK

APRON

THIS ISN'T ANY DIFFERENT FROM USUAL!

HUH? YOU'RE NOT HAPPY?

BUT WEREN'T YOU THE ONE WHO SAID YOU WANTED TO FALL IN LOVE WITH ME?

OH

...!

ARE YOU TIRED OF ME ALREADY?

OVER SOMETHING SO SMALL?

RUN! WINNIG NEW

I...

I never said I was tired of you...

IT'S JUST...

...I WISH WE COULD BE A LITTLE MORE ROMANTIC.

I THINK THAT'D BE NICE.

AH...

ROMANTIC, YOU SAY?
KRRK
THMP
LIKE THIS?
UH...!
UM...!

ZOOP
NOT LIKE THAT!
I MEAN LIKE THE DRAMA OF ROMANCE IN BOOKS AND FILM!
THIS ISN'T ROMANTIC AT ALL!
YOU DON'T KNOW THE FIRST THING ABOUT LOVE!
HMPH
OKAY.
...WHEN YOU GET BACK FROM SCHOOL, YOU TEACH ME WHAT LOVE MEANS TO YOU.
Pfft!
ON OUR NEXT DAY OFF...

BUT OF COURSE! JUST LEAVE IT TO ME!
WOO HOO. CAN'T WAIT.
(MONOTONE)
KRRK
SIT
YOU CAN GO BACK TO YOUR ROOM.
I HAVE TO THINK UP RECIPES.
IT'S ALL RIGHT.
I WANT TO BE HERE.

I LIKE WATCHING YOU CREATE RECIPES.
IT'S SO FUN TO IMAGINE WHAT KINDS OF SWEET TREATS YOU'LL COME UP WITH.
AND YOU'RE MY LOVER NOW, NATSU.
SO THAT MAKES MY LOVE FOR YOU ALL THE STRONGER.

...
THIS
THERE'S SO MUCH I DON'T KNOW.

THAT'S WHY I WANT TO LEARN.
EVERYTHING AND ANYTHING.
♡ MIKAMO CITY HARBOR PARK
WEDNESDAY, AFTER SCHOOL
SEE?
ISN'T THIS ROMANTIC?
NEAR...
FAR...
WHEREVER YOU ARE...
SOFT SERVE
IT'S A SCENE BETWEEN LOVERS FROM A MOVIE.
THE ONE WHERE THE BOAT SINKS.
Are you done yet?
UH-HUH.

HERE GOES...

BO

NK

You have an awfully weird way of drinking, Komomo-sama.

Ow...

Are we acting out Roman Holiday?

Maybe it's Cinderella?

?!

SO.

VHHR
HAS THIS BEEN ROMANTIC ENOUGH FOR YOU?
VHHR
VHHR
VHHR
...QUITE.
IT WAS JUST WHAT I WANTED.
Ho ho ho.
HM.
VHHR
IT DOESN'T MAKE ANY SENSE. WE TRIED ALL THE PRIMARY ROMANTIC SCENARIOS, BUT...
I had a most delightful time.
...IT DIDN'T GO AS I'D IMAGINED IT WOULD.
OKAY THEN.
SHALL WE TAKE THIS OPPORTUNITY TO KISS?
SHOCK
HUH?
WHAT'S WITH THAT REACTION?

YOU SHOULD BE ABLE TO KISS ME, DON'T YOU THINK?

OH

HUH? AREN'T WE SUPPOSED TO BE ALL ROMANTIC?

YOU'RE THE ONE WHO TRIED PLANTING ONE ON ME LAST TIME.

TH-THAT'S BECAUSE I THOUGHT I COULD DO IT!

NOW THAT WE'RE GOING OUT...

PREPARE YOURSELF. I'LL MAKE YOU CRY EVERY DAY.
EVIL FACE
THAT'S WHEN I REMEMBERED.

HE WOULDN'T HESITATE TO DO IT.
ARE YOU READY TO BREAK UP WITH ME NOW?
I CERTAINLY AM!
I COULD ENVISION THOSE HELLISH DAYS STARTING ALL OVER AGAIN.
OH
BUT IS LOVE SOMETHING THAT CAN BE ENDED SO ABRUPTLY?
I JUST AGREED TO BREAK UP.
NO. IT'S NOT.
THEN WHY...
YOU'RE NOT IN LOVE JUST BECAUSE YOU SAID YOU WOULD BE.
THAT'S BECAUSE THIS ISN'T LOVE.

THAT'S WHY IT'S SO EASY FOR YOU TO BREAK IT OFF.
BUT DOING THIS AGAIN...
...COULD REALLY HURT THE PERSON YOU'RE IN A RELATIONSHIP WITH.
DID I...HURT YOU?
ME?
I'M NOT HURT BY THIS.
...
BUT I'M STILL SORRY.
I WON'T DO IT AGAIN.

...
OKAY.
SO LONG AS YOU UNDERSTAND...
...THAT'S GOOD ENOUGH FOR ME.
THEN WITH WHOM...

...WILL I FIND LOVE?

HUH?

YOU BROKE UP?

YEAH.

I WAS PLANNING ON BREAKING UP WITH HER FROM THE VERY START.

LISTEN, NATSU...

HOW EXACTLY DO YOU FEEL TOWARD KOMOMO-CHAN?

...

AH!

I JUST THOUGHT OF A RECIPE FOR THE SUMMER.
VMP
I'LL BE IN MY ROOM.
KA-CHAK
...
THAT IDIOT.
WHAT IS HE THINKING?
THERE'S STILL SO MUCH...
SKRTCH
SKRTCH
23,5g
148 g
d'oeufs
...SHE DOESN'T UNDER-STAND.

I LIKE...
...WATCHING YOU CREATE RECIPES.

YOU DON'T...
...HAVE TO FALL IN LOVE WITH ME...
... KOMOMO-SAMA.

IT WILL ONLY MAKE YOU SAD.
I WANT TO FIND LOVE SOMEDAY.
I'M GOING OUT SHOPPING.
SERIE MÉLI-
CONFISERIE MÉLI-MÉLO
BUT I WON'T RUSH IT.
TAK
TAK
...I'LL MEET THE MAN OF MY DREAMS ONE DAY...
I'M SURE...
IT WILL BE A BEAUTIFUL ENCOUNTER.
SLIP
THUD!!
!!!
OW... UGH!
ARE YOU ALL RIGHT?
WAFT
I SMELL MINT...

AH.

GAPE GAPE

AH.

I'M SORRY, I COULDN'T HELP MYSELF. THIS SHOE...

...HAS A BROKEN HEEL.

YOU'D BETTER GET IT FIXED.

UH... MY SHOE?

BUT THESE ARE VERY FINE SHOES YOU HAVE HERE.

I HOPE YOU GET THEM REPAIRED RIGHT AWAY.

HMM.

ACTUALLY, WAIT RIGHT THERE.

I'LL FIX YOUR SHOE FOR YOU.

AH.
OH, YES.
TMP TMP TMP
HERE.
WEAR THESE UNTIL I CAN FIX THE HEEL.
WOW.
THEY SLID ON SO EASILY. THESE ARE SUCH NICE SHOES.
REALLY? THANK YOU. I MADE THEM.
FOR COMPLIMENTING MY SHOES, I'LL TELL YOU SOMETHING.
THEY SAY THAT A GOOD PAIR OF SHOES WILL BRING GOOD ENCOUNTERS.

I WONDER IF ONE OF THOSE ENCOUNTERS...
I WILL POUR MY HEART AND SOUL INTO REPAIRING YOUR SHOES...
...SO YOU CAN EXPERIENCE MANY SUCH ENCOUNTERS.
...WILL BRING LOVE.

CHAPTER 10
une crepe sil vous plait

I guess I should go on a trip...to a nearby dried-up riverbed!!

...
ALL RIGHT.
I'M SURE I CAN BUY THEM WITH THIS MONEY!
I WONDER WHAT A WONDERFUL ENCOUNTER IS LIKE.
TISERIE
HUH. YOU DON'T SAY.
SO KOMOMO-CHAN IS GETTING HER SHOES FIXED BY THAT SHOEMAKER SETO?
YEAH.
SHE SEEMED A LITTLE TOO EXCITED ABOUT THE WHOLE THING.
HEY, SO...
...WHERE IS KOMOMO-CHAN?

...WILL BUY HOWEVER MANY PAIRS OF SHOES IT TAKES TO HAVE A WONDERFUL ENCOUNTER TOO!
I WANT TO TOO!
...
KOMOMO... DID YOU BRING ANY MONEY?
I DID!
SHE'S GOING TO HIS SHOE SHOP WITH RISE KANAME TO PICK UP HER SHOES.
I WONDER WHAT IT WILL BE LIKE.
I...
Nivernais

JANGLE

I'VE BEEN SAVING UP A LITTLE EVERY DAY!

I JUST HEARD A JANGLE OF CHANGE.

THAT'S BECAUSE IT'S ALMOST ALL ¥500 COINS.

I should have guessed.

TODAY IS SUNDAY. I START WORK IN THE AFTERNOON.

SO THIS MORNING I'VE DECIDED TO GO TO THE SHOEMAKER WITH RISE.

AH!

SHOPPING WITH A FRIEND IS THE BEST!

Liberamente
calzolaio
THIS IS THE SHOP.
GET OUT!!
BAM
!!

OH.
SORRY I FRIGHTENED YOU.
GLARE
JOLT
I'LL LEAVE FOR TODAY.
BUT I'LL BE BACK.

S...
SORRY ABOUT THAT.
WE MET YESTERDAY. YOU'RE KOMOMO, RIGHT?
WELCOME TO MY SHOP.
Psst...
IN MY OPINION...
...IT'S NOT THAT ANGRY MAN FROM BEFORE, BUT IT'S THIS SHOPKEEPER WE SHOULD BE CAREFUL OF.

THE SHOES HERE ARE JUST LOVELY.
...
YOU THINK SO?
EITHER WAY, YOU WERE RIGHT.
I WONDER IF THAT MAN FROM BEFORE MADE THEM.
NOPE.
He's back!
THESE WERE ALL MADE BY MY MASTER.
He's in Italy right now.
I'M STILL LEARNING, SO I CAN'T SELL MY SHOES YET.
BUT I GET TO DO SIMPLE REPAIRS.
SHK
SHK
KOMOMO, I FINISHED FIXING YOUR BOOT.
Komomo?

¥76.000
¥63.000
SHK
Even with all I saved...
SHK
...I can't afford a single pair!
I never knew shoes were so expensive.
HUH?
YOUR BOOTS HERE ARE FAR MORE EXPENSIVE THAN THESE.
HUH?
THESE BOOTS ARE CUSTOM-MADE BY ITALY'S GREAT JOHN HOBB LINE.
THEY GO FOR ¥400,000 MINIMUM.
Whoever made this pair by hand has a custom shoe tree of your feet.

THESE AREN'T SOMETHING A HIGH SCHOOL GIRL LIKE YOU SHOULD BE WALKING AROUND IN.

THAT'S NOT TRUE!

BLOCK

KOMOMO USED TO BE A GLORIOUS RICH GIRL!

Not even I could compare!

RISE, STOP IT.

I'M NOT LIKE THAT ANYMORE.

BUT IT'S ODD THAT THOSE BOOTS SHOULD BE MORE EXPENSIVE THAN THESE.

I LIKE THE SHOES YOU MADE.

THAT'S WHY I CAME TO BUY ALL OF THEM WITH THE MONEY I SAVED UP.

...
KOMOMO, I'M JUST AN APPRENTICE.
I'M NOT SELLING ANY OF MY SHOES YET.
SO IF IT'S ALL RIGHT WITH YOU, WOULD YOU LET ME MAKE YOU A PAIR?
AND YOU CAN DECIDE THE PRICE FOR THEM YOURSELF.
...
JANGLE
I...
THIS IS ALL MY SAVINGS. IT'S PROBABLY ABOUT ¥10,000 TOTAL.
WILL THAT BE ENOUGH?
THAT'S PLENTY.

SO IN THE END...
...YOU ORDERED THREE PAIRS.
I'M SO GLAD HE HAD SUCH NICE SHOES!
HEE HEE HEE
THE OLD ME WOULD HAVE PROBABLY BOUGHT A RIDICULOUS NUMBER.
...
KOMOMO.
YES?
IS LIFE HARD FOR YOU NOW?
...? NOW? WHAT WOULD BE SO HARD ABOUT IT?
WELL...
YOU CAN BARELY AFFORD THINGS YOU USED TO BE ABLE TO BUY EASILY.

DO YOU EVER WISH...
...YOU COULD GO BACK?
BACK TO THAT?
ME ...?
TODAY'S TREAT: TARTE AUX POMMES (APPLE TART)
SO YOU ORDERED SOME SHOES?
Specialites

I DID. THEY WILL BE CUSTOM-MADE FOR ME.
FOR ONLY ¥10,000?!
THE SHOEMAKER I MET IS ONLY AN APPRENTICE.
SO HE SAID THAT ¥10,000 WAS MORE THAN ENOUGH.
TINK
HMM.
NATSU...
WHAT DO YOU MEAN?
DO YOU THINK I HAVE A HARD LIFE?
HUH?
THAT'S SOMETHING...

...ONLY YOU CAN ANSWER.
DO YOU THINK YOU HAVE A HARD LIFE, KOMOMO-SAMA?
...
NO. NOT AT ALL.
THEN THAT'S ALL THAT MATTERS.
BUT THINKING ABOUT IT...
DO I SEEM THAT WAY TO OTHERS?
...THERE HAVE BEEN LOTS OF PEOPLE...
...AFTER MY LIFE CHANGED WHO HAVE SAID...
..."IT MUST BE TOUGH" AND ASK ME, "DON'T YOU FEEL STIFLED?"
Agneau Pascal

Liberamente
...
SO THAT'S HIM.

IF ANYTHING HAPPENS TO HER, I'LL MAKE HIM PAY.
OH, KOMOMO JUST PASSED BY.
OH, YOU'RE RIGHT. I GUESS SHE'S WALKING HOME FROM SCHOOL.
That's her school uniform.
YOU KNOW KOMOMO TOO, SETO?
YES, SHE'S A CUSTOMER AT MY SHOP.
Did you hear?
HER FAMILY USED TO BE VERY WEALTHY.

BUT HER FATHER'S BUSINESS FAILED, AND NOW THEY HAVE NOTHING.
SHE DOESN'T LOOK THAT WAY TO ME.
THERE ARE SOME THINGS...
POOR CHILD.
IS SHE?
...THAT ARE INCONVE-NIENT ABOUT MY LIFE NOW...
KLAK
...BUT I WONDER ABOUT THAT.
Oh!
WELCOME, KOMOMO.
I CAME TO BE MEASURED.
RIGHT. PLEASE COME IN AND SIT.
I'M JUST GOING TO EAT LUNCH REAL QUICK.
MAYBE I'M DIFFERENT NOW.

BREAD!!
CUCUMBER!!
RRRIPPP
CHOMP
CHOMP
CHOMP
Seto, what on earth are you eating?
CHOMP
CHOMP
HUH?
CUCUMBER SANDWICH.
MRFF
THAT IS NOTHING LIKE WHAT A SANDWICH OUGHT TO BE!
It isn't!
THIS CANNOT BE TOLERATED!

IT'S ALL THE SAME ONCE IT GETS TO MY STOMACH.
IT IS NOT!
I...I CAN'T WATCH THIS ANYMORE.
I'M GOING BACK TO MÉLI-MÉLO TO MAKE YOU A GALETTE!
SO PLEASE EAT IT!
HUH? DON'T WORRY ABOUT THAT. LET'S START MEASURING YOUR FEET.
BE REASSURED THAT I MAKE A VERY FINE GALETTE.
FIRST LET'S GET YOUR FOOT MEASUREMENTS.
...
!!
PLOP
TOCK
TOCK

TOCK
TOCK
...
HE'S WORKING SO INTENTLY.
HE REMINDS ME OF NATSU.
Heh.
ARE YOU LIVING ON YOUR OWN NOW, KOMOMO?

YES, THAT'S RIGHT.
I DO EVERYTHING BY MYSELF NOW.
SOMETIMES NATSU HELPS TOO.
I GUESS...
...IT'S TRUE.
BUT FOR SOME REASON EVERYONE KEEPS THINKING I MUST HAVE IT SO TOUGH.
THEY ASK IF I WISH I COULD GO BACK TO MY OLD LIFE...
MY OLD LIFE WAS WONDERFUL.
BUT...
...AND INSIST THAT I MUST BE HAVING AN AWFUL TIME ADJUSTING.

YOU SEEM TO BE LIVING FREELY AND ENJOYING LIFE TO ME.
THAT'S RIGHT.

MY LIFE RIGHT NOW..
...IS VERY ENJOY-ABLE.
YOU'RE AMAZING, SETO.
HOW DID YOU KNOW HOW I FEEL?
HOW...?
KLANG
KLANG
THAT'S BECAUSE-
OH
SETO?

SHU...

YOU'RE COMING WITH ME TODAY.

OH.

YOU'RE...

...THAT MAN FROM THE OTHER DAY.

I BROUGHT THE OTHERS TOO.

LET'S GO.

YOU'RE COMING WITH ME, EVEN IF I HAVE TO DRAG YOU.

KOMOMO.

YOU WANT TO KNOW HOW...
...I KNOW WHAT YOU'RE FEELING?
...
I DO.
WELL THEN.
I'LL SHOW YOU.
MRMR
MRMR

BOW
YOU'VE BEEN MISSED, SHU-SAMA!

I'M...
...JUST LIKE YOU.
THE ONLY DIFFERENCE IS...
...I LEFT MY FAMILY TO PURSUE MY DREAM.

I'LL GET BACK TO FINISHING YOUR MEASUREMENTS...
...JUST AS SOON AS I KICK THESE PEOPLE OUT!

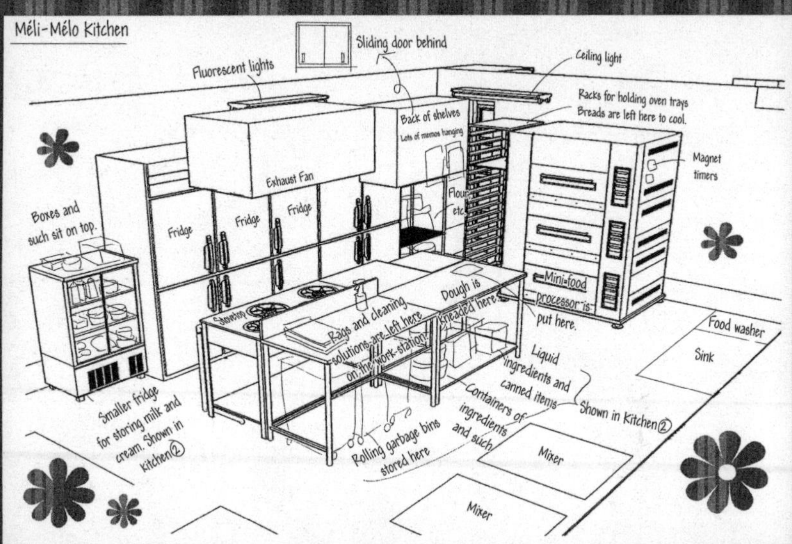

This page is devoted to the design of Méli-Mélo's kitchen!!
Myama-san made these so that when the assistants are drawing the kitchen, they know what goes where! There are so many appliances and such in a kitchen that it's a tough endeavor. I appreciate them always drawing such beautiful backgrounds for it!!

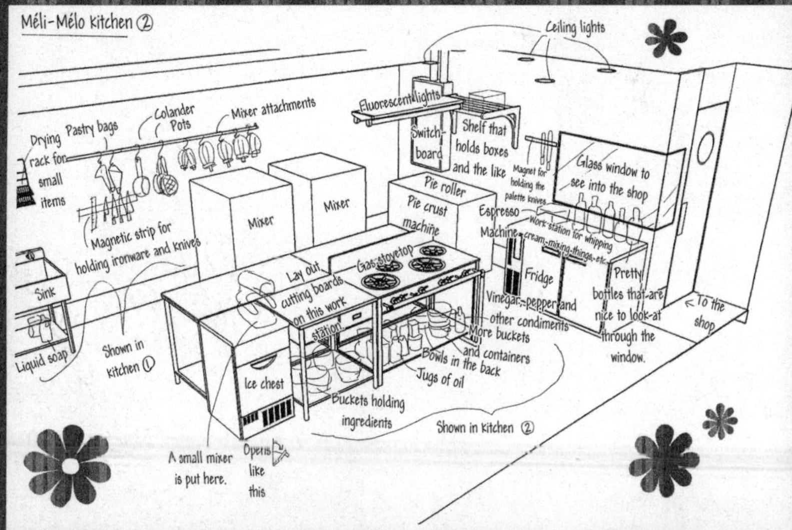

CHAPTER11

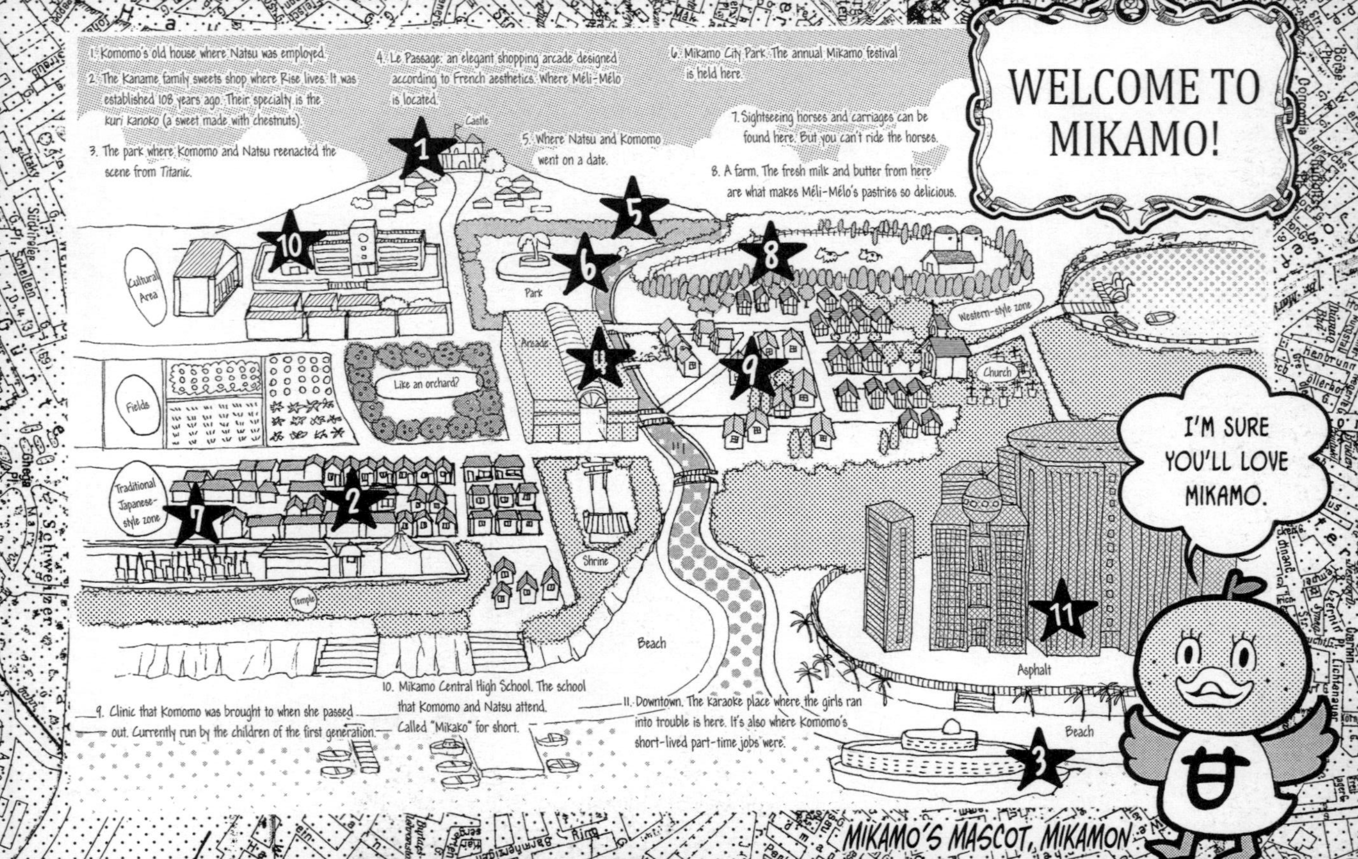
WELCOME TO MIKAMO!
1. Komomo's old house where Natsu was employed.
2. The Kaname family sweets shop where Rise lives. It was established 108 years ago. Their specialty is the kuri kanoko (a sweet made with chestnuts).
3. The park where Komomo and Natsu reenacted the scene from Titanic.
4. Le Passage: an elegant shopping arcade designed according to French aesthetics. Where Méli-Mélo is located.
5. Where Natsu and Komomo went on a date.
6. Mikamo City Park. The annual Mikamo festival is held here.
7. Sightseeing horses and carriages can be found here. But you can't ride the horses.
8. A farm. The fresh milk and butter from here are what makes Méli-Mélo's pastries so delicious.
9. Clinic that Komomo was brought to when she passed out. Currently run by the children of the first generation.
10. Mikamo Central High School. The school that Komomo and Natsu attend. Called "Mikako" for short.
11. Downtown. The karaoke place where the girls ran into trouble is here. It's also where Komomo's short-lived part-time jobs were.
Castle
Park
Arcade
Cultural Area
Fields
Like an orchard?
Traditional Japanese-style zone
Temple
Shrine
Western-style zone
Church
Beach
Asphalt
Beach
I'M SURE YOU'LL LOVE MIKAMO.
MIKAMO'S MASCOT, MIKAMON

⑥

• What I Like to Do Before Work These Days •

Before I start work, I doodle on a sheet of copier paper. It's fun just drawing whatever I want without having to worry about ever showing it to anyone. But lately, I've accumulated a lot of these sketches. I'm worried about where to keep them. I draw them with an Otona pencil, so they're very easy to create.

I HEARD YOU'D USE FORCE ON ME IF NECESSARY.
IF THAT'S THE CASE, THEN I'LL RESIST IN KIND.
SH-SHU-SAMA, WE WOULD NEVER HURT A HAIR ON YOUR HEAD!
WE WISH ONLY THAT YOU RETURN HOME.
TMP
THAT'S RIGHT, SHU!

ENOUGH OF THIS! COME AND CARRY ON THE FAMILY BUSINESS WITH ME, YOUR BIG BROTHER!
LOVE COMPLEX
I APOLOGIZE ON BEHALF OF MOTHER AND FATHER FOR DISOWNING YOU!
I ALREADY TOLD YOU, I'M NOT JOINING THE COMPANY. I'M LEAVING NOW.
Komomo, I'm ready!
GRAB
AND I'M ASKING YOU TO RECONSIDER!
LET ME GO–
EVERYONE.

IF SETO IS SAYING HE DOESN'T WANT TO GO...
...THEN WHY DON'T YOU JUST LEAVE HIM BE?
BESIDES, HE'S IN THE MIDDLE OF MAKING ME A PAIR OF SHOES.
PLEASE DO NOT DISRUPT US ANY FURTHER!
BAM!!

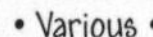

Here we are at the last sidebar. Thank you so much for following my story through all these pages.

I traded in my super-slow PC for a new super-efficient one. I just hope it lasts more than three years! Also, I think I'm going to try to get a driver's license this year.

I want to thank everyone who had a hand in the making of this book, starting with everyone who read it. Thanks also to my helpful assistants. My editors. Nakao-sama for helping me collect all my reference materials. Everyone at Tsujicho Cooking School. My friends. And my family.

-Maki Minami

My hearfelt thanks...

WHO IS THIS GIRL? She's so commanding...

THE REASON WHY SETO KNOWS HOW I FEEL...

...IS BECAUSE HE COMES FROM THE SAME CIRCUMSTANCES.

AND I KNOW HOW HE FEELS.

SHOES...?

WHO CARES ABOUT SOMETHING SO TRIVIAL?!

EXCUSE ME?

DID YOU...
...JUST SAY TRIVIAL?
I KNOW...
THE SHOES SETO MAKES ARE TRULY REMARKABLE.
DON'T YOU REALIZE?
I CHOSE HIM TO BE MY SHOEMAKER.

IF YOU'LL BE HEADING A COMPANY...
...YOU HAD BEST LEARN TO RECOGNIZE AND APPRECIATE AN EXCELLENT PRODUCT.
...WHAT SETO WANTS TO DO.

YOU UNDER-STAND WHAT I'M TELLING YOU?
URGH...!
SHE HAS...
...SUCH A SURPRISING INTENSITY...

I KNOW WHAT HE'S THINKING.
KOMOMO-CHAN SURE IS LATE.
ELI-MÉLO
YOU THINK SHE'S OKAY?
NATSU, DID YOU KNOW?
THEY SAY A GOOD PAIR OF SHOES...
...WILL BRING GOOD ENCOUNTERS.

IF ANYTHING HAPPENS TO HER...
I'LL
PAY.
SHOCK
HA HA...
HEH HEH HEH HEH
W-WHAT'S SO FUNNY?
SHE DIDN'T NEED...
...TO GET THOSE SHOES MADE.

I WAS JUST THINKING HOW HAPPY I AM...
I KNOW THAT SETO...
...TRULY ENJOYS THE LIFE HE LEADS NOW.
...TO HAVE SUCH A WONDERFUL CUSTOMER.
THAT'S WHY HE WON'T GIVE IN.
TMP
TMP TMP TMP

BROTHER, EVERYONE...
...PLEASE LET ME BE A SHOEMAKER.

BECAUSE HE'S DOING WHAT HE THINKS IS RIGHT FOR HIMSELF.
I BEG YOU.

AND YET... WHY?
HERE YOU GO.
I'M SORRY FOR GETTING YOU MIXED UP IN ALL THAT CRAZINESS.
...

THANKS.
...
GRMBL
IT SEEMS I'VE OFFENDED YOU.
I'M SORRY.
IT'S NOT THAT.
I'M JUST...
...A LITTLE DISAPPOINTED.
YOU DIDN'T DO ANYTHING WRONG.
YOU BOWED DOWN TO THEM. WHY?
HOW SO?
TO BOW DOWN TO SOMEONE ELSE...

BOWING DOESN'T MATTER...

I'LL DO WHAT IT TAKES TO ACCOMPLISH MY DREAM.

I'VE COMMITTED TO IT...
...SO I'LL DO ANYTHING.
ISN'T THAT WHAT ONE USUALLY DOES?

I...

OH, AND ALSO...

POFF
SUFF
THANKS FOR YOUR SPEECH IN DEFIANCE.
...DON'T UNDERSTA WHAT'S HAPPENIN

I DON'T KNOW WHY, BUT...
REEL

...I SUDDENLY FEEL...
...LIGHT-HEADED.

NATSU!
RRING
RRING
IT'S KOMOMO-CHAN!
CONFISERIE meli-melo
Traiteur
Epicerie
Specialites
AMETANI CLINIC
TMP
TM

FWISH

B-BMP
IF ANY-THING HAPPENS TO HER...
...I'LL...
AH.
KRRR

YOU MUST BE KOMOMO'S HOUSEMATE.
I'M SETO.
...
B-BMP
I'M SO SORRY...
B-BMP
BOW
...I LET THIS HAPPEN.
B-BMP
...

PLEASE DON'T APOLOGIZE.
I UNDERSTAND YOU INJURED YOUR ANKLE RESCUING KOMOMO.
BOW
I'M RELIEVED IT'S JUST A SPRAIN.
DON'T WORRY ABOUT IT. AS FOR KOMOMO ...
...SHE MUST FIND THE HOSPITAL RELAXING...
...BECAUSE SHE'S BEEN ASLEEP THE ENTIRE TIME.
IS SHE STILL ASLEEP?
EXCUSE ME?
WE HAVE AN EMERGENCY PATIENT COMING IN.
WE'LL NEED THE BED, I'M AFRAID...
Oh.
SURE.

IT'S ALL RIGHT.
I'LL CARRY HER.
IF ANY-THING...

...HAPPENS
TO HER...
...I'LL MAKE HIM PAY.

MM...

NATSU...?!

FINALLY.

YOU'RE AWAKE.

MY EYES MET SETO'S...

KOMOMO CONFISERIE VOL. 2/END

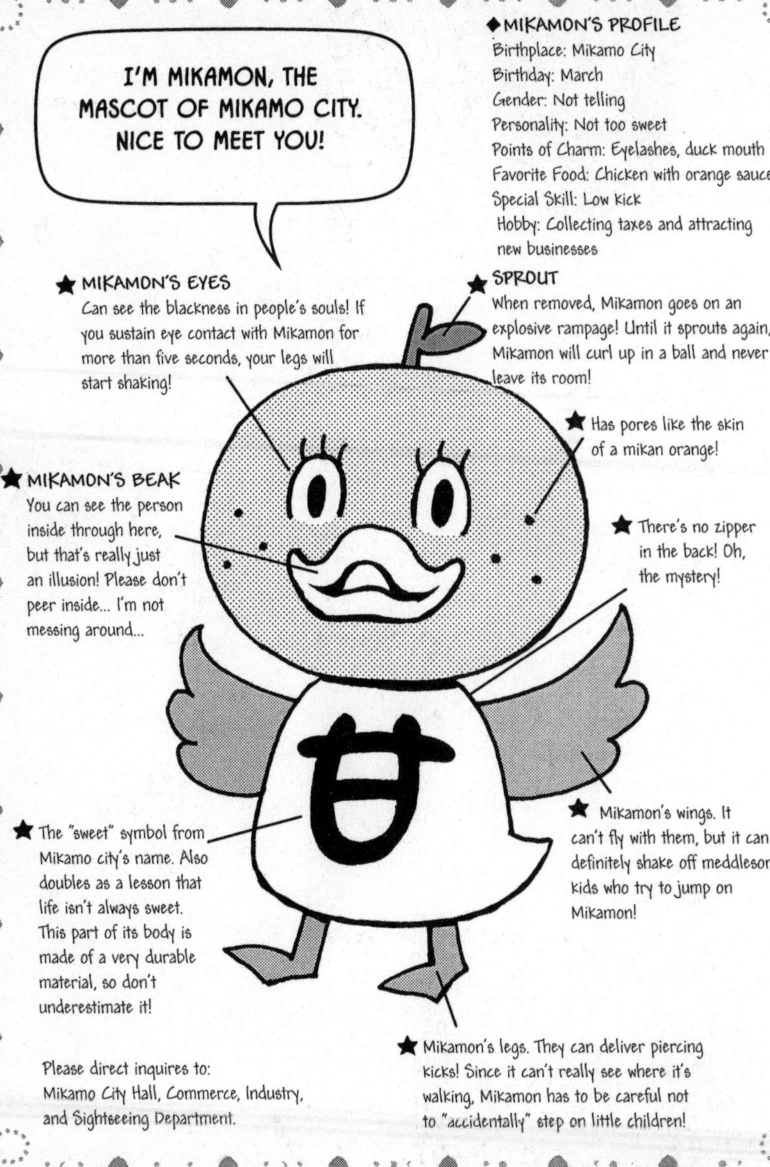
I'M MIKAMON, THE MASCOT OF MIKAMO CITY. NICE TO MEET YOU!
◆MIKAMON'S PROFILE
Birthplace: Mikamo City
Birthday: March
Gender: Not telling
Personality: Not too sweet
Points of Charm: Eyelashes, duck mouth
Favorite Food: Chicken with orange sauce
Special Skill: Low kick
Hobby: Collecting taxes and attracting new businesses
★MIKAMON'S EYES
Can see the blackness in people's souls! If you sustain eye contact with Mikamon for more than five seconds, your legs will start shaking!
★SPROUT
When removed, Mikamon goes on an explosive rampage! Until it sprouts again, Mikamon will curl up in a ball and never leave its room!
★Has pores like the skin of a mikan orange!
★MIKAMON'S BEAK
You can see the person inside through here, but that's really just an illusion! Please don't peer inside... I'm not messing around...
★There's no zipper in the back! Oh, the mystery!
★The "sweet" symbol from Mikamo city's name. Also doubles as a lesson that life isn't always sweet. This part of its body is made of a very durable material, so don't underestimate it!
★Mikamon's wings. It can't fly with them, but it can definitely shake off meddlesome kids who try to jump on Mikamon!
Please direct inquires to:
Mikamo City Hall, Commerce, Industry, and Sightseeing Department.
★Mikamon's legs. They can deliver piercing kicks! Since it can't really see where it's walking, Mikamon has to be careful not to "accidentally" step on little children!

~ MY PERSONAL TAKES ON DIFFERENT PASTRIES ~

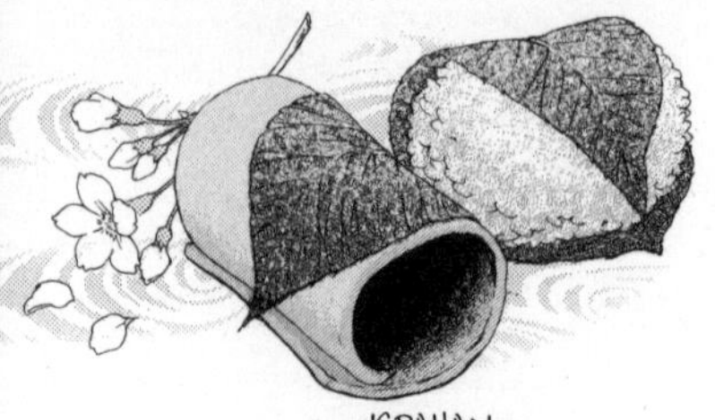

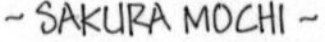

~ SAKURA MOCHI ~

It's wrapped in the leaf of a cherry blossom tree. Depending on the region it can vary, but where I live it's made of a light-pink colored confection and a sweet bean paste. It's called domyoji. It's one of the Japanese treats I crave on a regular basis.

~ ISPAHAN ~

An original cake made by Pierre Hermé. It consists of fresh lychee and raspberries sandwiched between rose macarons and crème. These ingredients don't really call to me, but when I finally tried one, I was surprised at how good it tasted. I'd like to eat it again some time. It really is a delicious and expensive cake. I bought this cake once only to leave it on the train. Aaaah!

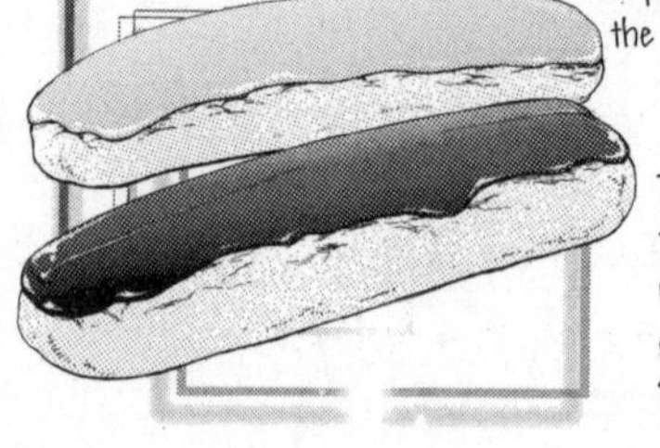

~ ÉCLAIR ~

The éclairs with fresh whipped cream and chocolate that they sell in French pastry shops make for a truly mouthwatering treat. I enjoy these, but I also really enjoy the custard éclairs they sell at convenience stores. So neener!

~ TARTE AUX POMMES ~

In short, it's an apple tart. I like to eat it with warmed vanilla ice cream chock full of vanilla beans and fluffy whipped cream on top. I also like when the apple has charred parts. Caramel! Caramel!

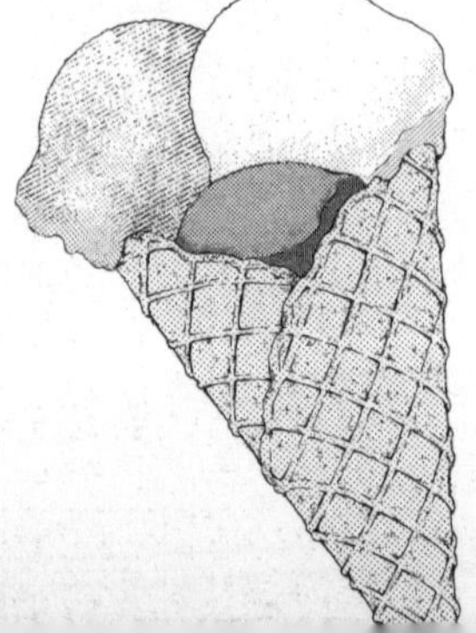

~ GELATO ~

Of all the many flavors you can get of this, I really love pistachio. It smells and tastes so good. And I love to eat it with the addition of salty caramel. It will make you fat. Hee hee!

BONUS PAGES

RISE & HER SERIOUS FRIENDS

WELCOME.

WOW, HE'S REALLY SMILING.

I'm frightened!

OH. THAT'S BECAUSE YOU'RE A CUSTOMER TODAY, KANAME.
AND SINCE KOMOMO-SAMA'S NOT AROUND, THERE'S NO POINT.
HUH?
I TEASE YOU IN FRONT OF HER...
WHY SHOULD I HAVE TO TORMENT YOU WHEN KOMOMO-SAMA ISN'T HERE?
...SO KOMOMO WILL SEE HOW MEAN I AM.
HIS SENSE OF LOVE IS MESSED UP.
I'M SUR-ROUNDED BY WEIRD PEOPLE.

AFTER ALL THE JOBS I'VE WORKED...

...I'VE ALWAYS WONDERED THIS.

THERE ARE TWO CLOCKS...

...OVER WHERE THEY KEEP THE HAMBURGERS AND FRIES.

ONE APPEARS TO BE FOR THE TIME ITEMS ARE MADE, BUT WHAT IS THE OTHER CLOCK USED FOR?

YAMADA.

IT'S ALREADY BEEN LONG ENOUGH, SO PLEASE THROW THOSE OUT.

YES SIR.

PLOP

PLOP

BONUS PAGES/END

Maki Minami is from Saitama Prefecture in Japan. She debuted in 2001 with *Kanata no Ao* (Faraway Blue). Her other works include *Kimi wa Girlfriend* (You're My Girlfriend), *Mainichi ga Takaramono* (Every Day Is a Treasure) and *Yuki Atataka* (Warm Winter). *S•A* and *Voice Over!: Seiyu Academy* are published in English by VIZ Media.

Komomo Confiserie
Shojo Beat Edition
Volume 2

STORY AND ART BY
Maki Minami

Supervisor: Tsuji Shizuo Ryori Kyoiku Kenkyujo/Hiromi Kosaka
Special thanks to Tsujicho Group

Translation/Christine Dashiell
Touch-up Art & Lettering/John Hunt
Design/Yukiko Whitley
Editor/Nancy Thistlethwaite

Komomo Confiserie by Maki Minami

First published in Japan in 2014 by HAKUSENSHA, Inc., Tokyo.
English language translation rights arranged with HAKUSENSHA, Inc., Tokyo.

Printed in the U.S.A.

Published by VIZ Media, LLC
P.O. Box 77010
San Francisco, CA 94107

10 9 8 7 6 5 4 3 2 1
First printing, December 2015

www.viz.com

www.shojobeat.com

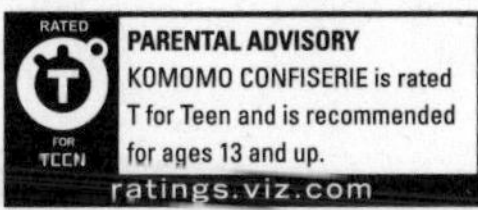

You may be reading the wrong way!

In keeping with the original Japanese comic format, this book reads from right to left, so action, sound effects and word balloons are reversed. This preserves the orientation of the original artwork. Check out the diagram below to get the order of things, and then turn to the other side of the book to get started!

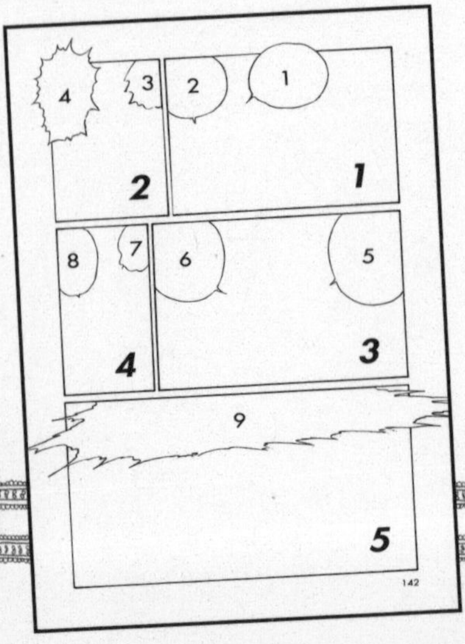